Stately, kindly, lordly friend
Condescend
Here to sit by me, and turn
Glorious eyes that smile and burn,
Golden eyes, love's lustrous meed,
On the golden page I read.

Algernon Charles Swinburne (1837–1909)
English poet

CATS DECOUPAGE BOOK

CONTENTS

velvet ears...

John Keats (1795–1821)
English poet

VICTORIAN CATS

The **Victorian age** was a golden one for cats. For the first time, cats were promoted from mere rat-catchers to admired and cosseted members of the family, with their own privileged position. British Victorians took the lead from their queen, who cherished a fine pair of Persians, and no Victorian hearth was complete without its own elegantly languorous feline. In the course of the 19th century, both Britain and America became nations of cat-worshippers. The very first cat shows took place at Crystal Palace in London in 1871, and in Madison Square Gardens in New York in 1895.

The Human Cat

Cats were seen to embody Victorian values more than any other animal. Childhood became romanticized during the 19th century, and attitudes towards certain pets, the cat chief among them, also became saturated in sentiment. Moreover, the rearing of pets was thought to be instructional in life skills for children: cats and children became natural companions, with the result that many Victorian cats suffered the indignity of petticoats and tea sets.

The impeccable maternal habits of the female cat were held up for praise in a society which staked much on its sense of duty and propriety. The innocent naughtiness of kittens was used to illustrate tracts on gentle but firm discipline. The dextrous hunting skills of cats were also admired: that symbol of imperial majesty, the lion, epitomised the peerless carnivore latent in his domesticated cousin blinking by the fire.

Louis Wain, the most famous Victorian cat artist, used cats to depict all the human virtues *and* the seven deadly sins. In Victorian art, the cat was seen as a great lover, and the amorous Tom was a most persistent feline Romeo, serenading his beloved from the rooftops, presenting her with Valentine cards or bouquets of flowers.

Conversely, cats were also depicted as the familiars of witches and part of Halloween's dark mysteries. But a black cat also came to symbolize good luck, especially when combined with a horseshoe.

The Clean and Cosy Cat

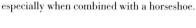

In the early 19th century, the advancement of science brought a new appreciation of physical as well as moral hygiene. The fastidious personal habits of cats were much approved in a society which liked nothing better than the suppression of unclean thoughts and deeds. Cats were also valued for their assistance, on a practical level, in exterminating the vermin that brought disease.

There was even a piece of furniture called the Cat — a double tripod used as a serving tray. It could not be knocked over as it would always balance on three of its six legs: no doubt a tribute to the real-life cat which would always land on its feet.

The Literary Cat

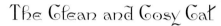

Many Victorian poets found an irresistible subject for their verse in their pet cats. Oscar Wilde, John Keats, Algernon Swinburne, Leigh Hunt and Alfred, Lord Tennyson all wrote adoringly about their feline friends. Many writers also acknowledged cats as their muses and indispensable desk companions. Charles Dickens had his Williamina. Christina Rossetti had her Muff, a half-Persian. John Greenleaf Whittier, Beatrix Potter and Mark Twain all enjoyed their cats, as did Harriet Beecher Stowe. In France, Théophile Gautier, Edmund Rostand, Champfleury and Charles Baudelaire wrote lovingly about cats.

INTRODUCTION

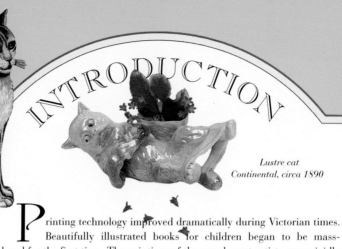

Lustre cat
Continental, circa 1890

Printing technology improved dramatically during Victorian times. Beautifully illustrated books for children began to be mass-produced for the first time. The paintings of the popular cat artists were vividly reproduced. Some of these delightful books also featured pop-ups or flaps to pull.

Juvenile literature was full of cat personalities—Puss in Boots, The Three Little Kittens of the eponymous nursery rhyme (see pages 40/41) and, of course, the enigmatic Cheshire Cat in Lewis Carroll's *Alice in Wonderland*. Rudyard Kipling wrote *The Cat that Walked by Himself.* Edward Lear firmly established the cat as a creature of luxury and romance in *The Owl and the Pussy Cat.*

The Decorative Cat

Cats were ubiquitous in Victorian gift wares—cards, money boxes, ink-wells, horseshoes and the ornaments which rewarded successful shots at fairground stalls. Some of these "fairings" are now valuable antiques.

In the wake of the Industrial Revolution, the toy industry boomed in Victorian Britain, America and Europe. A cat always took its place on the relevant alphabet block. Before teddy bears were popular there was a steady demand for stuffed cat toys, cat theatres, and cat "automata", metallic mechanical animals which could be wound up and made to walk or jump. Cats also starred in board games, jigsaw puzzles and on the glass slides of magic lanterns. Rocking cats and jointed cats were made out of cardboard.

Kittens and a mouse, oil on canvas, English, circa 1890

Earthenware moneybox
Staffordshire, early 20th century

VICTORIAN CATS

Earthenware plate, circa 1890, English

The oriental and southern edges of the British Empire brought in cat fans (see page 33). Japan was the home of automata. Germany and Austria specialized in small porcelain sculptures.

Cats were also used to enhance the attractiveness of everyday household objects. There were Puss in Boots gingerbread-cutters, black cat iron doorstops, cat dinner plates and cat candlesticks. Stylized felines also made their way on to samplers, woolwork cushions and hooked rag rugs. Cats made obvious cast-iron bird-scarers, sometimes with glinting glass beads for their eyes.

The Commercial Cat

Images of cats, the creatures of the hearth, the heart of the home, were often used to advertise household goods, such as furniture polish. The Globe cat pictured on this page was quite a favourite. Cats also "sold" matches, condensed milk, soap, sewing thread, chocolates and even tobacco (before it became associated with bad health).

Cats were often used to decorate trade cards, which were used not only for business but were also collectable in their own right, with the most attractive ones ending up in scrapbooks, along with postcards and other ephemera.

The Good Templars fairing 1880, Czech Springer and Oppenheimer

Cat band American, circa 1890

Good Templars

ASK FOR THE "GLOBE" POLISH AND SEE THAT YOU GET IT!

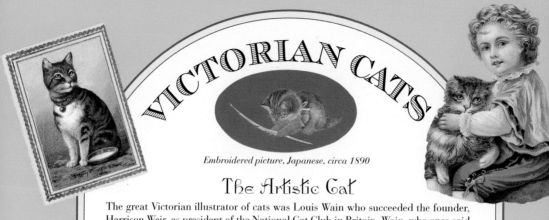

VICTORIAN CATS

Embroidered picture, Japanese, circa 1890

The Artistic Cat

The great Victorian illustrator of cats was Louis Wain who succeeded the founder, Harrison Weir, as president of the National Cat Club in Britain. Wain, who once said that he always started his cat pictures by drawing their ears, published a journal called Wain's Annual from 1901, entirely devoted to cats. His pictures showed wild and demented cats, lascivious and wicked cats, silly and sensible cats. Among his contemporaries, each with their own whimsical style, were Helena Maguire and Arthur Thiele. Harrison Weir, too, was a noted illustrator and also a writer about cats.

The Dutch-born painter, Henriette Knip (later Ronner-Knip), depicted them differently. Her beatific feline madonnas and their wide-eyed offspring were immensely appealing to Victorian sentimentality. In France, Louis Lambert was the great cat painter. Gottfried Mind, the Swiss artist, became known as the Raphael of cats.

The paintings of these artists were reproduced widely in magazines, books, calendars and, from 1870, on postcards, which were a collectable craze well into the 20th century. The popularity of cat images in the period between 1880 and 1920 was so great that the phenomenon came to be known as "Catland", a feline world populated with prettily-attired, well-equipped and trouble-prone animals, enacting all the rituals of daily life in imitation of their human creators.

Paper Tigers

Ever. before the advent of the postcard, cats were in demand on paper. Images of cats were widely available—as band-musicians, in mischievous combat with dogs and mice, in appealing poses with little girls—as Scraps. Victorian Scraps—sometimes known as chromos (short for chromolithographs) were brightly coloured, textured paper cut-outs which were used to decorate scrapbooks and all kinds of cards, including Valentine and Christmas cards. (Victorian Christmas cards were by no means restricted to snowy Santa scenes.) Scraps were also used to decorate boxes, screens and other furniture in the popular craft known as découpage, where a pattern of Scraps would be glued to a surface and varnished many times so that the images seemed painted on.

The earliest Scraps had appeared at the beginning of the 19th century, and one of the first companies to produce them was Mamelok, which was founded in Breslau in Germany in the late 1820s. Mamelok's Scraps are still in production today, often using the original images of nearly 200 years ago. Now in England, where the company moved in 1934, the Mamelok archive is the source of the cat Scraps used in the projects in this book, and also many of the images on these pages.

Victorian cat Scraps from the archives of Mamelok Press

A Note about Materials

The following materials are used for most of the projects in this book. Additional materials specific to a particular project are listed in the relevant sections.

- **Manicure scissors**
- **Small craft knife or scalpel**
- **Cutting mat or thick card**
- **P.V.A. or white glue**
- **Household sponge**
- **Brushes for painting, gluing and varnishing**
- **Water-based satin acrylic varnish**

General Notes on Cutting, Gluing, Painting and Varnishing

PAINTING

Water-based emulsion, latex or acrylic paints have been used for the backgrounds of the painted projects in this book and you can use whichever you have. The exceptions to this are the waste bin and table mat projects, where acrylic paint would not give the same result for the paint effects unless diluted with an acrylic glaze. Two coats of paint are always needed for good coverage. Make sure the first coat of paint is dry before applying the second. The time this takes depends on the surface being decorated. For example, the inside of the waste bin will take longer to dry than the outside which has a free circulation of air around it. Clean brushes with water immediately after use.

CUTTING

Some of the Scraps are only partially cut out and you will need to cut away any remaining pink or yellow background paper. You will also find that some of the Scraps look better when you cut away the backgrounds that the cats are placed upon: for example, those used to decorate the bookends and the waste bin. To achieve a good quality of work you will need to make sure that your scissors and scalpel or craft knife are nice and sharp. Use the knife to cut out small internal areas of paper like those on the pansy Scraps.

GLUING

P.V.A. or white craft glue is used for most of the projects, but when you are gluing on to a paper surface, for instance in the card project, you will get a neater result if you use a spray adhesive designed for craft work. You can buy this in most art stores. When using P.V.A./white glue for the painted projects, it is easier to brush it directly on to the surface being decorated, rather than the back of the Scrap, then place the Scrap over the glued area. It is essential to smooth out all bubbles of air from beneath the Scrap by pressing the paper firmly down and smoothing out the bubbles from the middle of the Scrap towards the edges. Clean off all traces of glue with a damp sponge immediately and let the project dry for at least two hours before varnishing.

VARNISHING

Water-based satin acrylic varnish, which is used in the projects throughout the book, dries very quickly, usually in about 20 minutes. However, you should allow at least two hours between coats unless otherwise directed by the manufacturer. Where between three and 10 coats are specified, the number you use is a matter of choice. The more you use, the smoother and more durable the result will be. This is particularly worth while for the waste bin, table mats and tea caddy, which are practical projects that will need to be handled. You do not need to sand between each layer of varnish, and unless you have used at least five coats you should not do so at all, otherwise you will damage the Scraps and reveal the white edges of the paper. If you have used more than five coats, for a smoother finish sand the varnish with a fine grade paper, before applying the final coat. If you prefer a matte look, brush on two final coats of matte varnish over the satin. Do not use this *instead* of satin varnish to build up several layers: if you do the result will be cloudy. A flat varnish brush for applying the varnish can be bought from art stores and is nicer to use than a household paintbrush. Clean all brushes in water immediately after use.

COSY CAT

A house without a cat, and a well-fed, well-petted, and properly revered cat, may be a perfect house, perhaps, but how can it prove its title?

Mark Twain (Samuel Langhorne Clemens)
(1835–1910) American writer

In Victorian times, images of cats were often used to decorate household objects, like this charming tea caddy, with its busy but delicate detailing of prints and beads. During the latter half of the 18th century, print rooms became popular in grand houses. Collections of prints were pasted directly on to the wall and surrounded by paper borders, swags and so on. This is the idea behind the pretty borders framing the cats, though the designs themselves are Victorian. This style of découpage is typically English. Both the borders and the painted background have been stained with tea to give an aged look.

TEA CADDY

Materials

YOU WILL NEED:

- Square tea caddy
- Scraps from sheet A111, A112, A120 and A125
- 5 photocopies of paper borders on pages 12/13
- White and pink paint (latex, emulsion or acrylic)
- Teabag
- Clear shellac or spray sealer for paper
- Repositionable adhesive
- Glass gemstones or acrylic jewels
- Strong, clear adhesive

1

Paint the tea caddy with two coats of white paint, letting the first coat dry before applying the second. Place the teabag in a cup and add a little boiling water to make a fairly strong brew. Brush the tea over the paintwork, let it dry, then brush on a further coat.

2

Brush the tea over the surface of the photocopies once. The paper is more absorbent than the paint and will take up more of the stain. When the paper is dry, seal the surface with clear shellac or spray sealer.

3

Cut out the borders and cats, and arrange them on the caddy, using repositionable adhesive to keep them in place. When you are happy with the positioning, mark the area between the border edge and the edge of the box that you paint pink. Remove all the Scraps and paint this area. It is better to paint an area slightly wider than you have marked to make absolutely sure none of the white paint shows after you have glued on the border.

4

Brush the surface of one side of the caddy with glue, and stick the borders and the cat in place. Where the borders overlap the lower part of the cat, the top and sides of the frame are glued on first, followed by the cat and finally the bottom section. The pink cord of the cat on the front is cut around and left unglued until the bottom border is in place so that it overhangs the frame. Clean off excess glue with a damp sponge and let it dry.

5

Brush the caddy with between three and 10 coats of acrylic varnish, depending on the quality of finish you require. Allow at least two hours between coats of varnish.

6

Add gemstones to decorate the top of your caddy using a strong, clear adhesive to prevent them becoming detached in use.

ROMANTIC CAT

You flirt with me as a concubine in robes of silk.

Amy Lowell (1874–1925) American writer

From our Cat Correspondent…

The Victorians often endowed cats and kittens with the human attributes of sentimentality and romance. Feline images were often used to decorate birthday cards and Valentines, so it is highly appropriate that one should decorate this handsome letter rack, an elegant repository for love letters!

The central section of this letter rack is removable, making it easier to decorate, and a rubber stamp has been used for the background pattern. The fleur-de-lis motif that has been used is, strictly speaking, medieval, but it often appeared in Victorian decoration. If you are unable to find a similar stamp, either choose an alternative motif or use a small stencilled pattern instead.

Embroidered cats, French, 19th century

LETTER RACK
Materials

YOU WILL NEED:

— Letter rack

— Scraps from sheets A123 and A125

   — Crimson latex, emulsion or acrylic paint

   — Metallic gold acrylic paint or ink pad

— Gilt cream/wax/gold leaf cream

— Soft cloth

— Rubber stamp or stencil

— Water-soluble pencil

— Ruler

On facing page:
Victorian lamp and writing accessories
Courtesy of The Cat Musuem

LETTER RACK
Step ❧ by ❧ Step

1

Paint all surfaces of the letter rack with two coats of crimson paint, letting the first dry thoroughly before applying the second.

2

Use a water-soluble pencil to draw a grid on the front and sides of the rack so that you can symmetrically place the fleur-de-lis. Ink the stamp by applying gold acrylic paint evenly to the rubber surface with a brush or using an ink pad. Carefully press the stamp on to the middle of each square. Wipe off the pencil marks when you have completed the stamped design.

3

Cut out the Scraps and glue them in place. Clean off excess glue with a damp sponge. Give the letter rack between three and 10 coats of varnish, depending on the result you require. Allow at least two hours between layers.

4

Apply gilt cream to the top and bottom edges of the letter rack, using a stiff brush to work it in well. Any smudged areas can be removed with white spirit/mineral spirits. Let this dry for a few hours before buffing with a soft cloth.

Stately, kindly, lordly friend
Condescend
Here to sit by me, and turn
Glorious eyes that smile and burn,
Golden eyes, love's lustrous meed,
On the golden page I read.

Algernon Charles Swinburne (1837–1909)
English poet

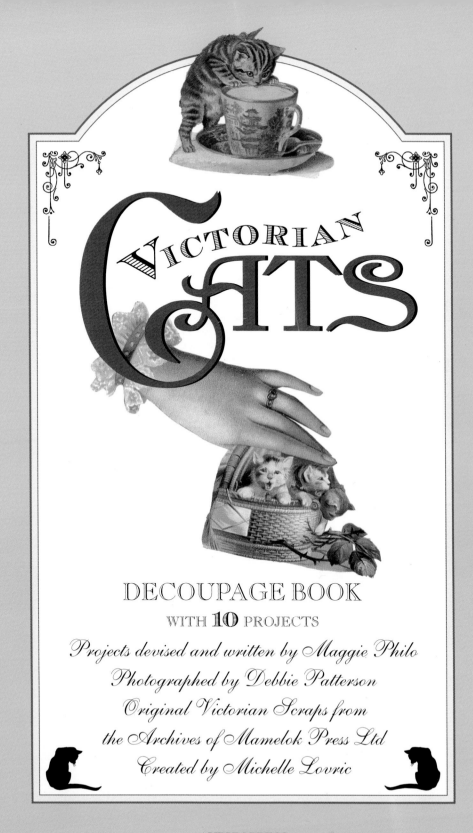

Victorian Cats

DECOUPAGE BOOK

WITH **10** PROJECTS

Projects devised and written by Maggie Philo
Photographed by Debbie Patterson
Original Victorian Scraps from
the Archives of Mamelok Press Ltd
Created by Michelle Lovric

AURUM PRESS

Gaze

Victorian

with those bright languid segments green, and prick tho

First published in 1997 by Aurum Press Ltd,
25 Bedford Avenue, London WC1B 3AT.
ISBN 1 85410 462 4

Edition
10
9
8
7
6
5
4
3
2
1

Concept, text and design © 1997 Michelle Lovric.

Project design and instructions © 1997 Maggie Philo.

Victorian Scraps © 1997 Mamelok Press Ltd.

Technical editors: Jean Kievlan and Carol Franklin.

Cover and portfolio design by Michelle Lovric and Lisa Pentreath.

Interior design by Michelle Lovric and Philippa Jarvis.

Step-by-step illustrations by Sally Launder.

Printed and bound in Singapore.

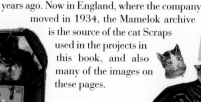

As o'er your fur
    I trail a negligible hand,
And gaze into your gazing eyes,
    And wonder in a demi-dream
What mystery it is that lies
Behind those slits that glare and gleam,
An exquisite enchantment falls
    About the portals of my sense...
O strange! For you are with me too,
And I who am a cat once more
    Follow the woman that was you.

Lytton Strachey (1880–1932)
English writer

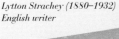

All your wondrous wealth of hair...
    Dark and fair,
Silken-shaggy, soft and bright
As the clouds and beams of night,
Pays my reverent hand's caress
Back with friendlier gentleness

Algernon Charles Swinburne
(1837–1909)
English poet

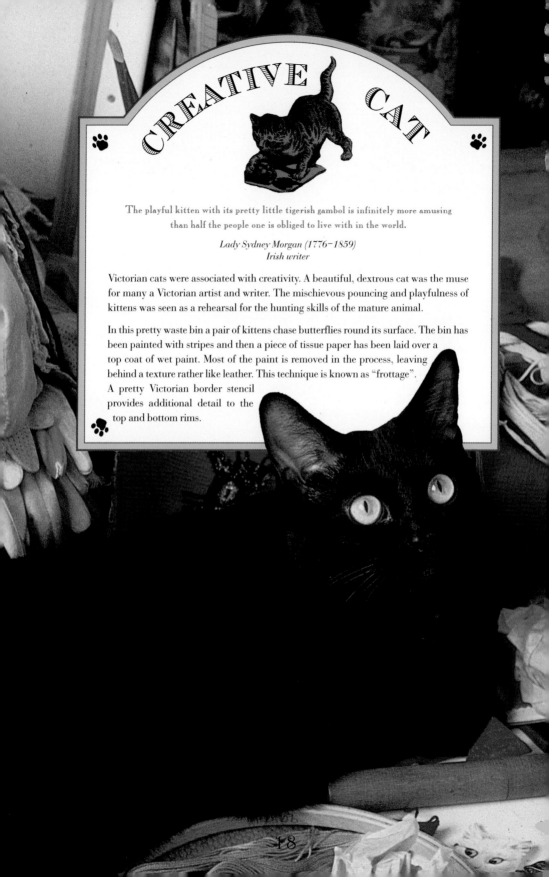

CREATIVE CAT

The playful kitten with its pretty little tigerish gambol is infinitely more amusing than half the people one is obliged to live with in the world.

Lady Sydney Morgan (1776–1859)
Irish writer

Victorian cats were associated with creativity. A beautiful, dextrous cat was the muse for many a Victorian artist and writer. The mischievous pouncing and playfulness of kittens was seen as a rehearsal for the hunting skills of the mature animal.

In this pretty waste bin a pair of kittens chase butterflies round its surface. The bin has been painted with stripes and then a piece of tissue paper has been laid over a top coat of wet paint. Most of the paint is removed in the process, leaving behind a texture rather like leather. This technique is known as "frottage". A pretty Victorian border stencil provides additional detail to the top and bottom rims.

WASTE BIN

Materials

YOU WILL NEED:

- Metal waste bin
- Scraps from sheets A121, A122, and A123
- Metal primer
- Olive, medium and dark green latex or emulsion paint
- Masking tape
- Tissue paper
- Stencil film or acetate
- Stencil brush
- Metallic gold acrylic paint
  - Kitchen paper or paper towels
  - Repositionable adhesive

Pert as any young page-boy, the small black cat
Plays on my table, and has the freedom of it;
And there quite motionless sometimes he will sit,
For all the world like a dainty live paper-weight.

Not a hair on his black pelt moving,
    without a stir,
He rests there long, dead-black on a white leaf,
Like a little toy cat, whose lolling tongue—
A soft felt pad—serves for pen-wiper.

Edmond Rostand (1868–1918)
French writer

WASTE BIN

1 Paint all surfaces of the bin with a metal primer according to the manufacturer's instructions. When it has thoroughly dried, brush the dark green paint inside the bin and olive green on the outside. Two coats will be needed for both. Let paint dry thoroughly.

2 Use masking tape to divide the bin into equal sections. Paint alternate sections with the medium green paint and let it dry.

3 Brush a coat of dark green paint over the stripes and immediately press a piece of tissue against the wet surface and peel off. Quickly continue around the bin before the paint starts to dry. This should leave the surface with a textured effect that resembles leather.

A KITTEN IS SO FLEXIBLE THAT SHE IS ALMOST DOUBLE; THE HIND PARTS ARE EQUIVALENT TO ANOTHER KITTEN WITH WHICH FOREPART PLA

Step ❖ by ❖ Step

*Henry David Thoreau
(1817–62)
American writer*

SHE DOES NOT DISCOVER THAT HER TAIL BELONGS TO HER UNTIL YOU TREAD ON IT...

4

5

6

Trace the stencil design on to the stencil film or acetate and secure in place on the bin with masking tape. Dip the stencil brush into the gold paint, then blot it on a piece of kitchen paper or a paper towel, so that only a minimum of paint remains on the brush. Apply this to the stencil with a dabbing motion. Continue in this way until the design is completed all the way round.

Cut out the cats and butterflies, and arrange them around the bin using repositionable adhesive to hold them in place. When you are happy with the design, remove one Scrap at a time, brush the surface of the bin with glue and stick the Scrap firmly in place. Extra care needs to be taken in removing air bubbles from the large cat Scraps. Clean off excess glue with a damp sponge.

A waste bin needs to be especially durable so apply three coats of acrylic varnish to the inside surface and five or more on the outside as a final touch.

CURIOUS CAT

The Victorian cat, like its ancestors and descendants, was famous for its inquisitive nature. In this project, cats decorate a document box which *could* be the repository of the family secrets…

This box has been cleverly designed to look like a book, so the sides have been painted to look like gold-edged pages. If you are decorating a more traditional shaped box you may prefer to paint it the same shade on all sides. The finished design has been painted with dark shellac. This has a yellowing effect and resembles work produced in the Victorian era. The all-over style of découpage is one that was much used during this time.

DOCUMENT BOX

Materials

YOU WILL NEED:

- Document box
- Scraps from sheets A111, A112, A119, A120, A121, A122, A124 and A125
  - Dark green and crimson shades of latex, emulsion or acrylic paint
  - Brown shellac
- Ribbon measuring approx. 2 ft (60 cm)
- Metallic gold marker pen
- Masking tape
- Ruler
- Repositionable adhesive

DOCUMENT BOX
Step ❧ by ❧ Step

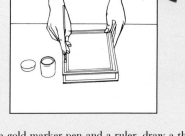

1

Paint the box dark green on the outside and crimson on the inside. Make sure the first coat is thoroughly dry before applying the second.

2

Using a gold marker pen and a ruler, draw a thin gold line just inside the edge of the lid. Mask off $\frac{1}{4}$ in (7 mm) band inside the gold line and paint this with crimson paint. Draw another gold line to outline the inside of the crimson border.

3

Cut out the Scraps and try different arrangements on the lid, using a repositionable adhesive to hold the Scraps in place. When you are happy with your design, remove the Scraps at the top, brush glue in their place, then press the Scraps back firmly into position. Continue in this way down the box, taking extra care that the cats are well stuck down where the paper overlaps. Clean off the excess glue with a damp sponge and let it dry.

4

Varnish the box with as many layers of varnish as you require, allowing two hours for drying between each coat. Next, brush on one or two coats of brown shellac, and let the first dry thoroughly before applying the second. If you have a suitably shaped box, glue a piece of ribbon to each half to complete the look.

HISTORICAL NOTE: Cats and Hallowe'en

The beautiful enigma of cats had its dark side. Black cats, the familiars of witches, have always been associated with Hallowe'en, an ancient Celtic festival which marked the time when ghosts, devils and witches were supposed to haunt the earth, bringing mischief and mayhem in their wake. The chief events are supposed to take place around October 31 each year: All-Hallows Eve.

By Victorian times, witches were taken much less seriously and cats were no longer in danger of being stoned to death, drowned or of other forms of persecution which had been a risk in earlier times.

"And I," said Miaow, lifting up her voice, "I am the horror and haunter of the night season. When I pass like the night wind over the roofs of the houses men shudder in their beds and tremble. When they hear my voice as I creep stealthily along their balconies they cry to their gods for succor. They arise, and from their windows they offer me their priceless household treasures—the sacred vessels dedicated to their great god Shiv—which they call 'Shivin Mugs'—the Kloes Brøsh, the Boo-jak, urging me to fly them! And yet," said Miaow mournfully, "it is but my love song! Think ye what they would do if I were on the war-path."

Francis Bret Harte
(1836–1902)
American writer

Black cat doorstop

Gunmetal painted horseshoe trivet
English, early 20th century

SLEEPY CAT

In reverie they emulate the noble mood
Of giant sphinxes stretched in depths of solitude
Who seem to slumber in a never-ending dream...

Charles Baudelaire
(1821–67)
French writer

CLOCK FACE

Most cats need 24 hours a day sleep, and some cats need more, as the old saying goes. In this project, a curled-up cat decorates a crackle-glazed clock face. What more restful way to watch the hours pass?

There are several *craqueleur* (crackling) kits on the market, including new water-based ones, and if you use these you will need to follow the manufacturer's instructions accordingly. The one used here consists of a slow-drying oil-based varnish followed by a fast-drying water-based varnish. This is still the type most widely available. If cracks do not appear after the second of the coats of varnish is dry, put the clock near a source of heat, such as a radiator, or use a hairdryer on a low heat setting held at some distance. This last coat is water soluble, so care must be taken not to get it wet or touch the surface with damp hands. White spirit/mineral spirits should be used to clean off oil-based varnish and paints from brushes.

CLOCK FACE

Materials

YOU WILL NEED:

— Clock kit

— Photocopy of a decorative clock face

— Scraps from sheets A112 and A123

— White and purple latex, emulsion or acrylic paint

— 2-part *craqueleur* (crackling) kit

— Raw umber artists' oil paint

— Oil-based satin or matte varnish

— White spirit/mineral spirits

— Soft-haired synthetic brush

— Kitchen paper, paper towels or soft cloth

Step ❧ by ❧ Step

1

Paint the clock with two coats of white paint, then paint the edges with a shade of purple that matches the pansies.

2

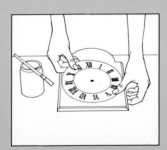

Brush glue on to the surface of the clock and stick on the photocopied face. Carefully smooth out all bubbles of air, working from the middle of the paper towards the edges. Clean off excess glue with a damp sponge.

3

Cut out the Scraps, and glue the pansies on to each corner and the sleeping cat to the top part of the clock. Wipe off excess glue and let the clock dry thoroughly. Apply between three and 10 coats of satin acrylic varnish.

Brush on the first coat of oil-based crackling varnish. Let this dry for between two and four hours, until it feels dry when you gently wipe a finger over the surface, but is still tacky when you press the back of your knuckle to it. Brush on the second water-based part, making sure that you cover all the area that has been painted with the oil varnish. A soft-haired synthetic brush works best for this. This second coat of varnish should be dry in about half-an-hour.

Dilute a squeeze of raw umber artists' oil paint with a little white spirit, then rub this into the surface of the clock with a piece of kitchen paper, a paper towel or soft cloth. Then, using a clean piece of paper or cloth, wipe away the excess paint to reveal the cracks. Any areas that missed the second coat will appear as a brown mark. If this happens, use a little white spirit/mineral spirits to remove them. Let the clock dry overnight.

Seal the surface of the clock with one or two coats of satin or matte oil-based varnish.

Beautiful present sufficingness of a cat's imagination! Confined to the snug circle of her own sides, and the two next inches of rug or carpet.

Leigh Hunt (1784–1859), English writer

29

WEDDING CAT

An enduring image of Victorian times is that of a beautiful and innocent young girl holding a kitten. Many Scraps depicted such a scene, and for this project one of the most appealing has been chosen. This picture keepsake is exactly what might be found on the dressing table of a young lady about to be married.

A tortoiseshell frame is not only historically relevant, but seems rather apt for a picture featuring a cat. Genuine tortoiseshell becomes transparent when polished and lacquer painted on the surface beneath gives it a glowing opacity. A vermilion shade was sometimes used and does look very striking, but the yellow seen on this frame is more customary. The effect has been achieved by combining the traditional decorative paint techniques of rag rolling and vinegar graining. If you are unable to obtain pure powdered pigment, you can use acrylic paint diluted with water instead, but the markings will not be as pronounced. Oval doilies can be found fairly easily, but if you have difficulty obtaining one, you could paint a pale blue line around the child instead.

The Owl looked up to the stars above,
And sang to a small guitar,
"O lovely Pussy! O Pussy, my love,
What a beautiful Pussy you are,
You are,
You are!
What a beautiful Pussy you are!"

Edward Lear (1812–88)
English painter and poet

PICTURE KEEPSAKE

Materials

YOU WILL NEED:

— Picture frame
— Scrap from sheet A124
— Golden yellow latex emulsion or acrylic paint
— Burnt sienna and burnt umber powder pigment
— Small chamois leather or cotton rag
— Vinegar and sugar
— Masking tape
— Fine grade sandpaper
— Cream textured paper to fit frame
— Oval doily
— Pale blue acrylic paint
   — Satin or gloss acrylic varnish
   — Clear shellac or spray sealant
   — Spray adhesive

PICTURE KEEPSAKE

1

Paint the frame with two coats of golden yellow paint. Seal the paint with two coats of acrylic varnish. This makes it easier to clean off any mistakes.

WOMAN and CAT

They were at play, she and her cat,
And it was marvellous to mark
The white paw and the white hand pat
Each other in the deepening dark.

The stealthy little lady hid
Under the mitten's silken sheath
Her dainty agate nails...

Paul Verlaine (1844–96)
French poet

2

Add a teaspoon of sugar to half a cup of vinegar and mix well. This quantity will keep for a couple of months in a screw-top jar. Take a teaspoonful each of burnt sienna and burnt umber pigment, and add enough vinegar mix to each shade to make a liquid but opaque paint. Use masking tape to section off two diagonally opposite ends of the frame. Paint the other two corners with the vinegar paint, or with watered-down acrylic paint if using this substitute method.

3

Lightly gather a length of damp chamois leather or cotton rag into a sausage shape and immediately roll this diagonally over the wet paint.

Step ❖ by ❖ Step

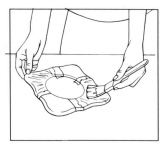

4

Use a very soft brush to disperse some of the paint by brushing first in the direction that you rag rolled, then across it. Let it dry, then brush on a coat of clear shellac or use a spray sealant. When this has dried, repeat this process over the same sections with the burnt umber paint. Remove the tape, and mask the opposite corners. Complete the frame in the same way, this time rolling the leather in the other direction. Let it dry thoroughly. To complete the tortoiseshell effect, give the frame three or four coats of varnish. A gloss varnish will give a nice glassy effect. Smooth the surface with a fine grade sandpaper, then apply a final coat of varnish.

Handpainted silk fan circa 1885, probably French colonial African

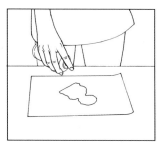

5

Cut out the child and kitten, and also a piece of textured paper to fit inside the frame. Place the Scrap face down on a piece of paper to protect the work surface and spray the back with adhesive. Then stick the Scrap in place on the textured paper.

6

Paint an oval doily with pale blue paint and let it dry. Carefully cut out the middle section so that what remains leaves a pretty paper lace border surrounding the child. Trim the edges of the doily to fit the paper background and glue in place using a spray adhesive. Place the picture inside the frame.

BIRTHDAY CAT

I was only a kitten, and I was too frisky to know about time.
But I grew faster than the rose-buds did.

Frances Hodgson Burnett (1849–1924)
English-born American writer

Even in Victorian times, cats knew all about having a good time. These picturesque party animals were often shown celebrating human-style. Here, a combination of cat portraits and miniature scenes of cat life are used to decorate festive napkin rings for an alfresco birthday party.

These napkin rings have been made from empty shampoo bottles. The end of a scalpel knife is used as a template to draw the scalloped edge. Brass and aluminium metal leaf are used to decorate the surface which gives the wonderful glow to the tissue paper. The leaf is transferred to acrylic goldsize and because this stays tacky indefinitely the napkin rings can be gilded after about 15 minutes or even the next day. If you would prefer a simpler project, use a good quality gold or silver acrylic paint instead.

NAPKIN RINGS

Materials

YOU WILL NEED:

— **Empty plastic bottles**
— **Scraps from sheets A111 and A119**
— **Marker pen**
— **Curved template**
— **Transfer metal leaf (aluminium and brass)**

— **Acrylic goldsize/foil leaf adhesive**
— **Metallic gold and silver acrylic paints**
— **Soft-haired synthetic brush**
— **Tissue paper**

NAPKIN RINGS

1

Cut the plastic bottles into strips slightly larger than 2 in (5 cm) wide. Hold a marker pen steadily in your hand and use a support to raise its height if necessary. Hold the pen against the strip of plastic and turn this slowly round, drawing an even line around it. Mark a second line about $\frac{1}{4}$ in (7 mm) above the first. Turn the plastic strip upside down and repeat the process. Trim away the plastic at both ends of the ring up to the first line.

2

Use the end of a scalpel or craft knife, a small coin or other suitable item and draw a curved line in between the two lines at each end of the ring. Cut around the curved shape with a pair of sharp scissors.

Step ❧ by ❧ Step

3

Paint the inside of each ring with either gold or silver paint, then brush acrylic goldsize on the outside. Let this dry until it has become clear—about 15 minutes.

4

Cut a strip of metal leaf slightly wider than the napkin ring, and press this around the tacky goldsize. Apply metal leaf until all surfaces of the ring are completed.

5

Cut a strip of tissue paper about $1\frac{1}{2}$ in (3.8 cm) wide and long enough to fit around the ring. Brush the surface of the ring with glue and carefully stick the tissue around it.

6

Cut out the cat Scraps and glue them on to the surface of each ring. Brush a coat of glue over the top to seal.

The Kittens' Tea Party by Walter Potter
photograph copyright © Stefan Richter 1996 All rights reserved/ reproduction prohibited

LITERARY CAT

Cats have always been the intellectuals among household pets, equally at home among the poets and the novelists. In the schoolroom, their irreproachable family life and personal habits were thought to be instructional. In this project, an enchanting pair of white kittens are used to decorate a pair of bookends which might have graced a child's desk and consoled him for going "Back to School".

If you have difficulty finding suitable bookends, don't worry: they can be very easily made from plywood or M.D.F. You will need to use wood/M.D.F. with a depth of $\frac{1}{2}$ in (1.2 cm) and cut two pieces measuring 4 x 4 in (10 x 10 cm), two measuring 4 x $3\frac{1}{2}$ in (10 x 8.8 cm), and two measuring approx. $1\frac{1}{2}$ x $1\frac{1}{2}$ in (3.8 x 3.8 cm). Spread glue along the bottom of one side of the 4 x 4 in (10 x 10 cm) squares and butt the other two larger pieces against these to form a right angle. Hold them in place with sticky tape until the glue has set. The two smallest squares can then be glued to the base of the bookends to support the cat figure.

A PAIR of BOOKENDS

Materials

YOU WILL NEED:

- Pair of bookends
- Scraps from sheets A119 and A120
- Light blue paint latex emulsion or acrylic paint

- Blue and pink latex, emulsion or acrylic paint to match the cats' ribbons
- Thick card
- Brown antique wax

BOOKENDS

1

Paint the bookends with two coats of light blue paint, letting the first coat dry thoroughly before applying the second. Next, paint the edges of the bookends using pink paint, decorating the half that the blue cat will sit upon. Use blue paint for the bookend on which the pink cat will perch. Varnish the bookends with three or more coats of acrylic varnish.

2

Apply a brown antiquing wax to the bookends to give them an aged look. Avoid the front of the little square that will support the cat as glue will not adhere to a waxed surface.

Dogs may fawn on all and some
As they come;
You, a friend of loftier mind,
Answer friends alone in kind.
Just your foot upon my hand
Softly bids it understand.

*Algernon Charles Swinburne
(1837–1909), English poet*

**The three
Little Kittens.**

Step ❀ by ❀ Step

3

Cut out the cat figures and glue them to thick card. Cut away excess card surrounding the cat with a sharp scalpel knife.

4

Paint the back of each Scrap with light blue paint, then apply two coats of varnish to both sides of the cats and glue them in place against the supports.

GREEDY CAT

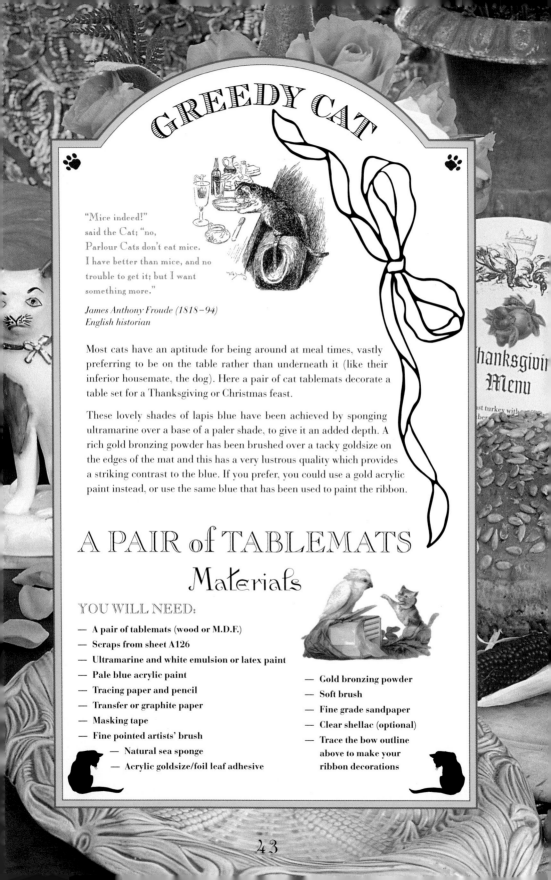

"Mice indeed!"
said the Cat; "no,
Parlour Cats don't eat mice.
I have better than mice, and no
trouble to get it; but I want
something more."

James Anthony Froude (1818–94)
English historian

Most cats have an aptitude for being around at meal times, vastly preferring to be on the table rather than underneath it (like their inferior housemate, the dog). Here a pair of cat tablemats decorate a table set for a Thanksgiving or Christmas feast.

These lovely shades of lapis blue have been achieved by sponging ultramarine over a base of a paler shade, to give it an added depth. A rich gold bronzing powder has been brushed over a tacky goldsize on the edges of the mat and this has a very lustrous quality which provides a striking contrast to the blue. If you prefer, you could use a gold acrylic paint instead, or use the same blue that has been used to paint the ribbon.

A PAIR of TABLEMATS
Materials

YOU WILL NEED:

— A pair of tablemats (wood or M.D.F.)
— Scraps from sheet A126
— Ultramarine and white emulsion or latex paint
— Pale blue acrylic paint
— Tracing paper and pencil
— Transfer or graphite paper
— Masking tape
— Fine pointed artists' brush
    — Natural sea sponge
    — Acrylic goldsize/foil leaf adhesive

— Gold bronzing powder
— Soft brush
— Fine grade sandpaper
— Clear shellac (optional)
— Trace the bow outline above to make your ribbon decorations

A PAIR of TABLEMATS
Step • by • Step

1

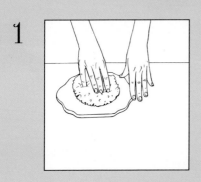

Make a light blue paint by mixing the white and ultramarine blue paints together. Paint the mats with two coats of this shade. Brush one coat of the darker blue on to one of the mats and immediately dab the surface all over with a damp sponge. Complete the other mat in the same way.

2

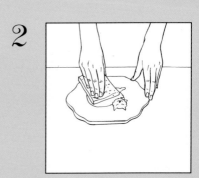

Cut out the cat Scraps. Brush glue on to the middle of each mat and place a cat in the middle. Smooth out any bubbles of air towards the edges of the paper. Clean off excess glue with a damp sponge and let it dry for at least two hours.

3

Trace the ribbon design on page 43 and place it in position on the mat. Slide a piece of transfer or graphite paper underneath and hold the tracing paper in place with masking tape. Trace over the design to transfer the ribbon to the mat.

WHEN YOU ASCEND THE SCALE OF BEING, AND COME TO AN ANIMAL THAT IS, LIKE OURSELVES, INEDIBLE, YOU HA

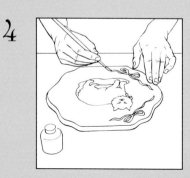

Fill in the ribbon design using a fine brush and light blue acrylic paint to match the ribbon around the cat's neck.

5

Apply three or more coats of satin acrylic varnish to each mat, allowing at least two hours between each coat. Smooth the last layer of varnish with a fine grade sandpaper, then give it a final coat.

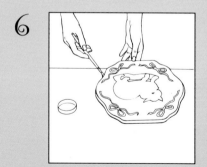

6

Brush acrylic goldsize around the edges of each mat and leave it for about 15 minutes until it has become clear. Use a soft brush to dust the gold powder over the tacky size. If you like, you can make the gold edges of the mat more durable by brushing on one or two coats of clear shellac.

Charles Dudley Warner
(1829–1900)
American essayist and novelist

...RIVED AT A RESULT WHERE YOU CAN REST! LET US RESPECT THE CAT, HE COMPLETES AN EDIBLE CHAIN...

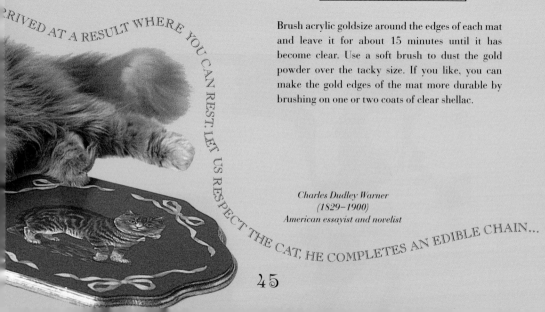

CHRISTMAS CAT

The Victorians did not confine themselves to robins and reindeer for their cuddly Christmas imagery. Cats were often depicted in Christmas cards. In these projects, Victorian cat Scraps are used to decorate an address book, a special card and a gift tag.

Marbled papers were commonly used to bind Victorian books, and this type of paper is now widely available and often sold as gift wrap. The beautiful and typically Victorian-looking brown paper used for these projects has been hand marbled, while the pretty blue one is mass produced. Apart from when the marbled paper is glued to the cover of the address book, spray adhesive should be used throughout for these projects, instead of P.V.A. or white glue, to prevent the card and paper from becoming stained, or too wet or crinkled.

ADDRESS BOOK, CARD & GIFT TAG
Materials

YOU WILL NEED:

- Address book approx. 4¼ x 6 in (11 x 15 cm)
- Scraps from sheets A111, A112 and A124
- Sheet of brown marbled paper
- Sheet of blue marbled paper
- Sheet of peacock blue card
    - Heart-shaped doily
    - Metallic gold acrylic paint
    - Metallic gold marker pen
- Tracing paper
- Soft pencil
- Transfer paper (optional)
- Spray adhesive
- Gold ribbons and Christmas trimmings
- Ruler
- Fine pointed artists' brush
- Double-sided sticky pad, adhesive tape or dots

CHRISTMAS CARD

Step • by • Step

1

Cut a piece of peacock blue card approx. 14 x 7½ in (36 x 19cm) and a piece of brown marbled paper the same size. Stick the marbled paper over the card, let it dry, then fold the card in half. Cut a second piece of card approx. 5½ x 6¼ in (14 x 16cm) and draw a line around the edge using a gold marker pen and a ruler.

2

Glue the card in place, making sure that the surrounding marbled border is equal on all sides. Paint the heart-shaped doily with gold acrylic paint. When it is dry, stick it on the front of the blue card, using the spray adhesive, and position the cat Scrap in the middle of the background area.

3

Trace the holly leaf design here and scribble on the back of the tracing paper with a soft pencil. Turn the paper over again and trace the design on to each corner of the card. Or you can use a piece of transfer paper beneath the tracing. Fill in the design with gold acrylic paint and a fine brush, and attach the trimmings with a double-sided sticky pad.

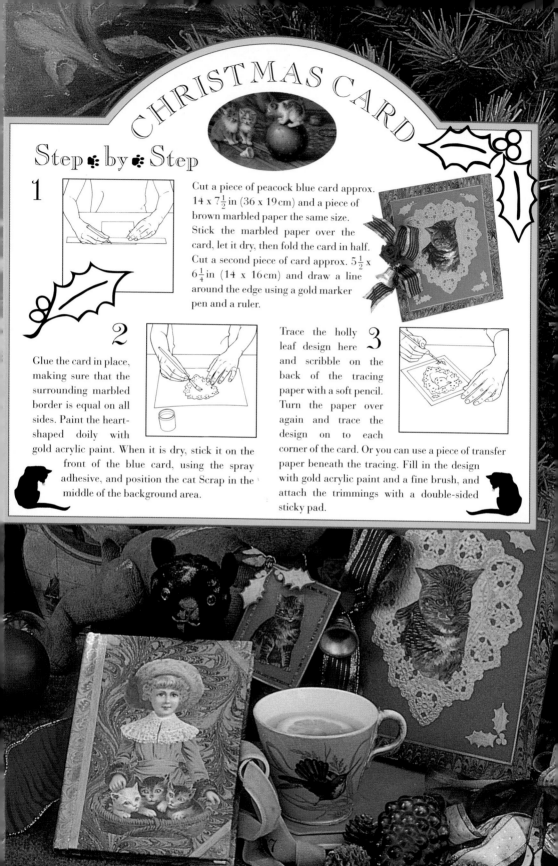

ADDRESS BOOK
Step ❧ by ❧ Step

1

Lay the address book open over a sheet of brown marbled paper. Cut a piece about $\frac{1}{2}$ in (1.2 cm) larger on all sides and allow extra for the width of the spine. Cut away the paper at the corners and in the middle so that the edges can be neatly folded inside the cover.

2

Brush the back of the paper with glue and stick it over the cover of the book, folding over the edges and securing these on the inside. Let it dry, then cut out and stick the little girl with her basket of cats on the front. Cut out the blue marbled paper to decorate the spine and corners and glue these in place.

3

Allow the cover to dry thoroughly, then glue on a narrow band of gold ribbon adjacent to the blue paper and two equal lengths of ribbon to the inside cover of the book.

GIFT TAG

Cut a piece of peacock blue card approx. 3 x 4 in (7.5 x 10 cm). Outline the edges with a gold marker pen, then cut very narrow strips of marbled paper to form a border around the cat. Glue the border and the cat Scrap in place. Glue on the trimmings to complete the tag. You can also make additional holly leaves as shown here.

About the Victorian Scraps...

The Victorian Scraps and Victorian Stand-up Cat featured in this book are available from Mamelok Press Ltd. For further information about the Scraps and for details of all stockists, please write to Mamelok Press Ltd, Northern Way, Bury St Edmunds, Suffolk IP32 6NJ, England, telephone 01284 762291, facsimile 01284 703689. Victorian Scraps from the Mamelok archive are available in the United States from Artifacts Inc., 3120 West Oak Street, Palestine, TX 75801 USA, telephone 1-903 729 4178.

About this book...

Victorian Cats is the third kit in this unique and highly successful series, each kit comprising a beautifully illustrated project book plus all the Victorian Scraps needed to make every design. The first book, *Victorian Découpage*, has sold over 100,000 copies in six languages. The second book in the series, *Victorian Christmas*, includes a history of 19th-century Christmas customs.

About the authors...

MAGGIE PHILO is a highly successful découpage designer, interior decorator and author. With her extensive knowledge of specialist paint finishes, she is in demand as an interior designer, and has been profiled in decorating magazines and exhibited at important interior design shows. This is her fifth book about découpage and she has also made a video about découpage techniques. Maggie is married with five children and lives in Brighton.

MICHELLE LOVRIC creates specialist books for major publishers. She has compiled illustrated anthologies, produced kits of books and cards, written children's stories and designed themed ranges of cards. Her book, *Love Letters — AN ANTHOLOGY OF PASSION*, was a *New York Times* bestseller. Michelle lives and works in Covent Garden, London.

JEAN KIEVLAN is a partner in the creative services design team of Kievlan-McGuffee of Fort Worth, Texas. An accomplished designer, Jean has authored over 150 craft "how-to" books, appeared on numerous television craft shows and works with manufacturers in the craft industry to develop new products.

The editor gratefully acknowledges the cooperation of Tiggly, Fluffball and Chintzy, and their owners, Michel Thivet and Louise Levison, and of Macduff, and his owners Bill and Fiona McCreadie, and finally, of Gamoush, for his footprints. Please note that none of the cats suffered any discomfort or inconvenience in order to achieve these photographs. In fact, they appeared to enjoy themselves. The editor also gratefully acknowledges the following sources for the items used in photography: for most of the antique cat objets d'art, pictures and toys, The Cat Museum, 49 High Street, Harrow on the Hill, Middlesex HA1 3HT, telephone 0181 422 1892, with many thanks to Kathleen Mann for all her help. For antique clothing, shawls and accessories from Lunn Antiques Ltd, 22 Cucumber Alley, Thomas Neal's, Shorts Gardens, Covent Garden, London WC2. For antique textiles for interiors, Lunn Antiques Ltd, 86 New Kings Road, Parsons Green, London SW6 4LU. For numerous small but essential props, Yvonne Dawe and Debbie Patterson. For the blanks of the Document Box, Picture Frame and Clock, Decorative Arts Co., 5a Royal Crescent, London W11 4SN, telephone 0171 371 4303. For the blanks of the Table Mats and Letter Rack, Scumble Goosie, Lewiston Mill, Brimscombe, Stroud, Glos., telephone 01453 731305. Many thanks, too, to Joan Piercy, for her kind help with the cutting out of Scraps.

The Kittens' Wedding and The Kittens' Tea Party tableaux by Walter Potter can be seen at Potter's Museum of Curiosity, Jamaica Inn, Bolventor, Bodmin Moor, Cornwall PL15 7TS, telephone 01566 86838.

LEAVE ME WITH A GESTURE OF INCONCEIVABLE IMPUDENCE, CONVEYED BY THE VANISHING QUIRK OF YOUR TAIL

Amy Lowell (1874–1925)
American poet